HISTORIC BUILDINGS
OF
WASHINGTON, D.C.

A Coloring Book
of Architecture

by Scott Clowney

Commonwealth Editions
Carlisle, Massachusetts

To Liam and Conner—may your imaginations take you to unexpected places.

Special thanks to the National Building Museum for countless opportunities afforded to me since 2004. This institution—this home away from home—has changed my perspective on the building arts. Thanks to my family and friends for their steadfast support and belief in me. I am forever grateful. Also thanks to Michael Higdon and the team at Applewood Books.

978-1-938700-48-4

Text edits by Kristen Sheldon and Stephanie Dabek

The display type is Petit Four, created by David Kerkhoff in 2015.

Published by Commonwealth Editions, an imprint of Applewood Books, Inc., P.O. Box 27, Carlisle, Massachusetts 01741

Visit us on the web at www.commonwealtheditions.com
Visit Scott Clowney on the web at www.scottclowney.com

Printed in the United States of America

INTRODUCTION

Has architecture ever made you pause in wonderment? Do you ever consider why buildings look a certain way, how buildings were constructed, or what stories buildings could tell? Are you ever curious about the interplay of materials, patterns, shapes, and space? Well, I am, and the building arts continue to inspire me and pique my curiosity.

Since 2004, I've had the privilege of calling Washington, D.C., my home and, nearly overnight, fell in love with the city's diverse and vibrant culture. As years progressed, I explored city neighborhoods and discovered a melting pot of architectural building types: decorative historic buildings such as the Smithsonian's Arts and Industries Building; unadorned modern buildings such as the Third Church of Christ, Scientist (now razed); and eccentric contemporary buildings such as St. Coletta of Greater Washington. With such a rich and evolving architectural history, I enjoy drawing and illustrating the city as a means of documenting my encounters.

The majority of drawings in my collection represent buildings in the northwest quadrant, where I live, work, and play. Above all, I'm drawn to intriguing structures that captivate the eye and tug at my heart: quaint Victorian row houses, streamlined Art Deco office buildings, and grand Neoclassical government buildings. On warm sunny days, I trek through city streets to observe and sketch buildings in the field. On cold or rainy days, I stay indoors to analyze and draw buildings from photos. For the purpose of this coloring book, each building was photographed on-site by me, then carefully transferred to paper to create a pseudo realistic impression.

Whether you're a novice or an expert, I hope you enjoy these drawings and come to appreciate the rich architectural history of our nation's capital. I hope this book inspires you to explore this great city in new and fun-filled ways.

—Scott Clowney

CONTENTS

U.S. CAPITOL DOME

LOCATION: **East Capitol Street NE
and 1st Street SE**
NEIGHBORHOOD: **Capitol Hill**
ARCHITECT: **Thomas U. Walter**

The U.S. Capitol dome is 289 feet high, made of cast iron with an inner and outer dome, and topped with a 19-foot-high bronze statue known as *Freedom*. Completed in 1866, this dome replaced a previous dome designed by Charles Bulfinch, Third Architect of the Capitol.

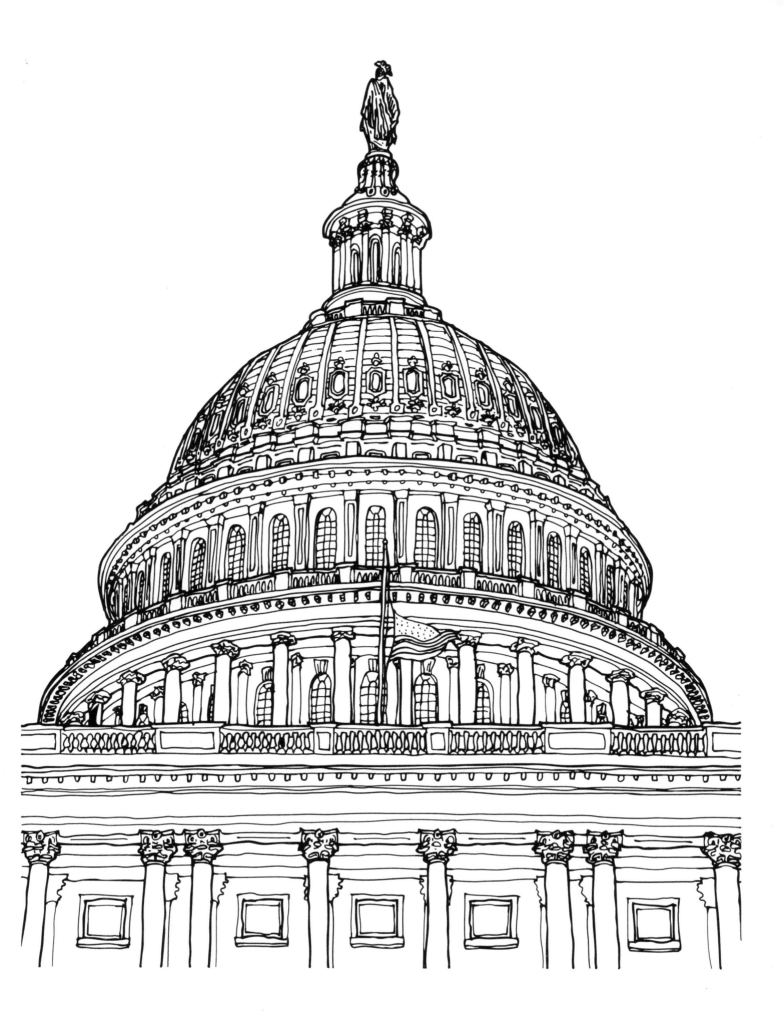

CHRISTOPHER COLUMBUS MEMORIAL FOUNTAIN, UNION STATION

LOCATION: Massachusetts and Louisiana Avenues NE
NEIGHBORHOOD: Capitol Hill
ARCHITECT: Daniel H. Burnham & Lorado Taft (Sculptor)

This marble monument was completed and dedicated by President Taft in 1912. Depicting Columbus' voyage to the New World, this monument is ornate with sculptures of King Ferdinand and Queen Isabella of Spain and a Native American with his bows and arrows. Columbus' statue faces the Capitol building.

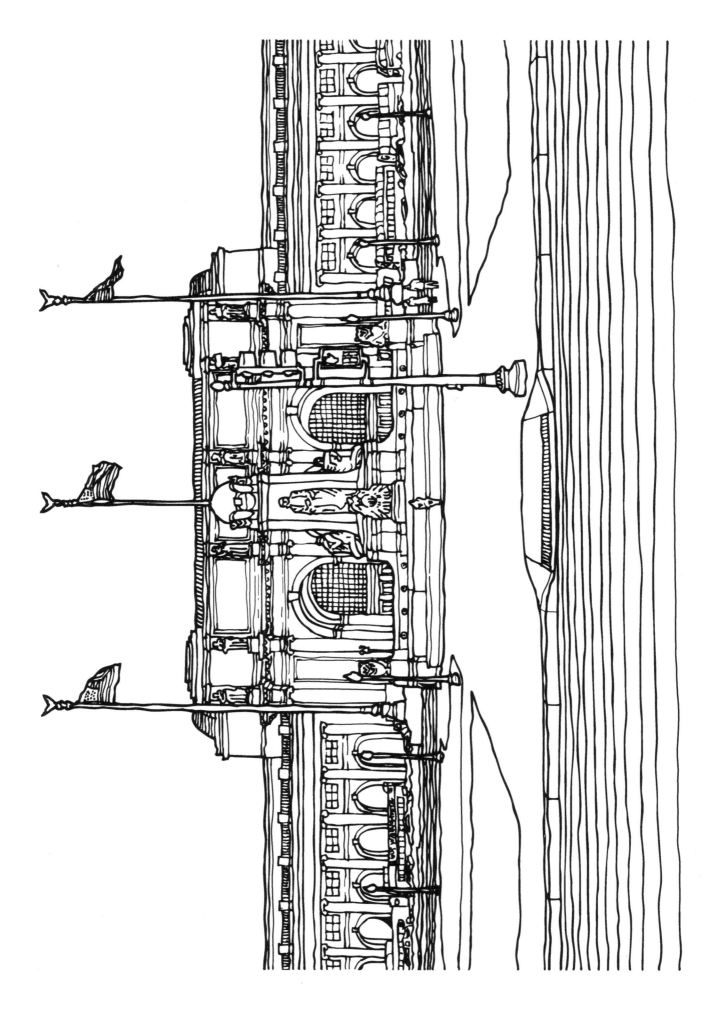

U.S. SUPREME COURT

LOCATION: **1 1st Street NE**
NEIGHBORHOOD: **Capitol Hill**
ARCHITECT: **Cass Gilbert**

President Herbert Hoover laid the cornerstone in 1932 for the U.S. Supreme Court. The building is decorated by Roman influences such as porticoes with elaborate pediments and a raised plinth on which the building rests.

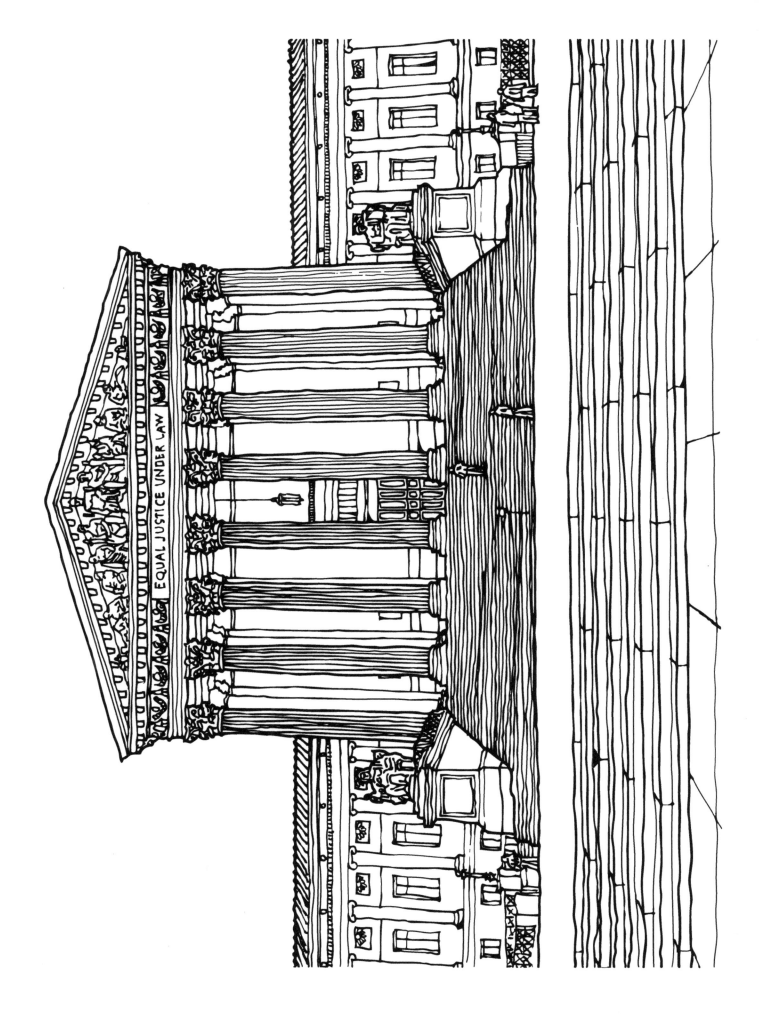

JEFFERSON BUILDING, LIBRARY OF CONGRESS

LOCATION: **10 1st Street SE**
NEIGHBORHOOD: **Capitol Hill**
ARCHITECTS: **John L. Smithmeyer and Paul J. Pelz**

The Library of Congress was built in response to the 1814 invasion in which the British burned the small library being housed in the Capitol. Surpassed in holdings only by the British Library, the Library of Congress houses more than 162 million catalogued items.

FREDERICK DOUGLASS HOUSE

LOCATION: **1411 W Street SE**
NEIGHBORHOOD: **Anacostia**
ARCHITECT: **John Van Hook**

Frederick Douglass nicknamed the home where he lived for 17 years Cedar Hills as an homage to the trees that surrounded the property. Upon his death in 1895, Douglass' widow and the U.S. Congress established the Frederick Douglass Memorial and Historical Association (FDMHA) at the site of the home. It opened to the public in 1903 and was taken over by the National Park Service in 1962.

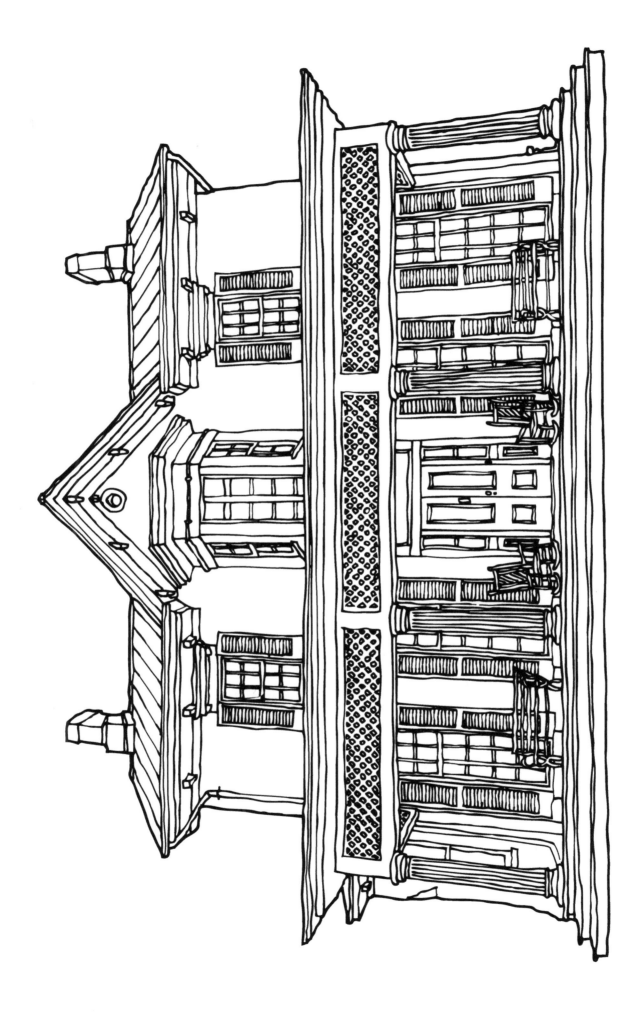

SMITHSONIAN INSTITUTION BUILDING, THE CASTLE

LOCATION: **1000 Jefferson Drive SW**
NEIGHBORHOOD: **National Mall**
ARCHITECT: **James Renwick Jr.**

James Smithson, a scientist from Britain, left in his will upon his death in 1829 that money be given to the United States—a country he had never visited—to establish an institution for knowledge. Designed as the original Smithsonian Museum in 1855, this structure housed the first collection, which contained live owls and animals, like bison, that grazed the south yard of the Castle. Smithson was reburied inside the Smithsonian Castle in 1904.

THOMAS JEFFERSON MEMORIAL

LOCATION: **701 East Basin Drive SW**
NEIGHBORHOOD: **Tidal Basin**
ARCHITECT: **John Russell Pope**

Aligned with the White House in a north-south axis, the memorial was dedicated in 1943 and contains 54 columns, a domed roof reaching 129 feet, and a 19-foot-tall bronze statue of Thomas Jefferson. Notable quotes by Jefferson are displayed inside, including excerpts from the Declaration of Independence, which he wrote in 1776.

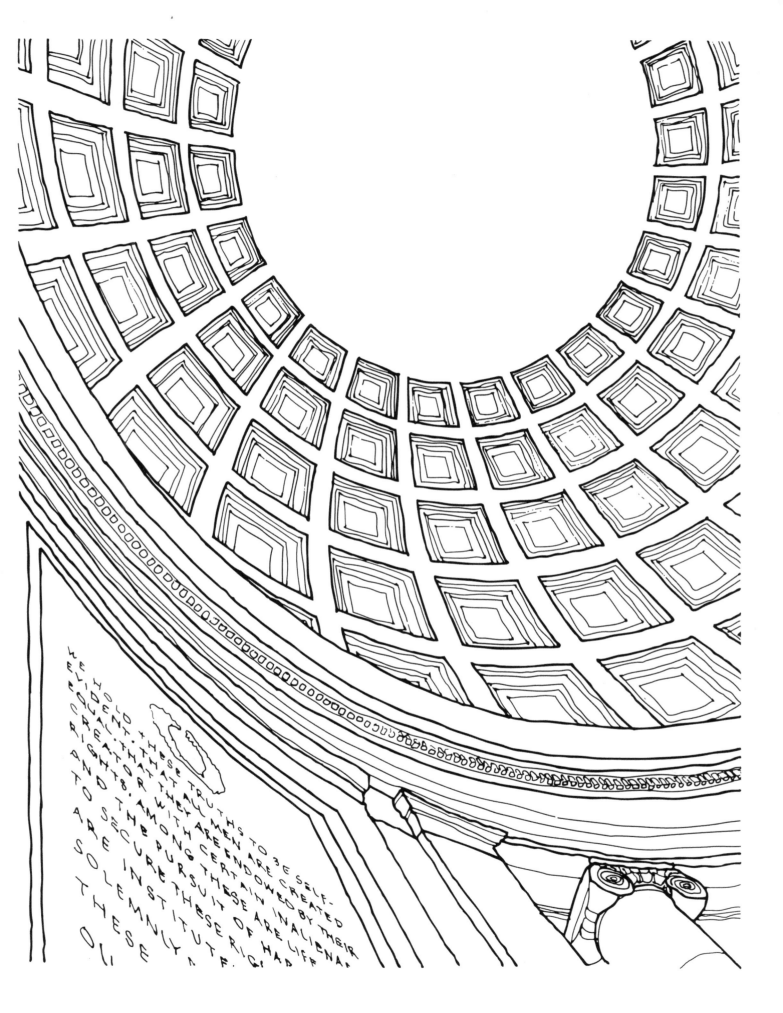

WASHINGTON MONUMENT

LOCATION: **2 15th Street NW**
NEIGHBORHOOD: **National Mall**
ARCHITECT: **Robert Mills**

A monument to America's first president, George Washington, this 555-foot-tall marble and granite obelisk contains more than 190 interior memorial stones. Although construction began in 1848, the Civil War caused a halt in construction, which can be seen one-third of the way up as the color of the stone is slightly changed. The Washington Monument was officially completed in 1884 with the placement of the capstone.

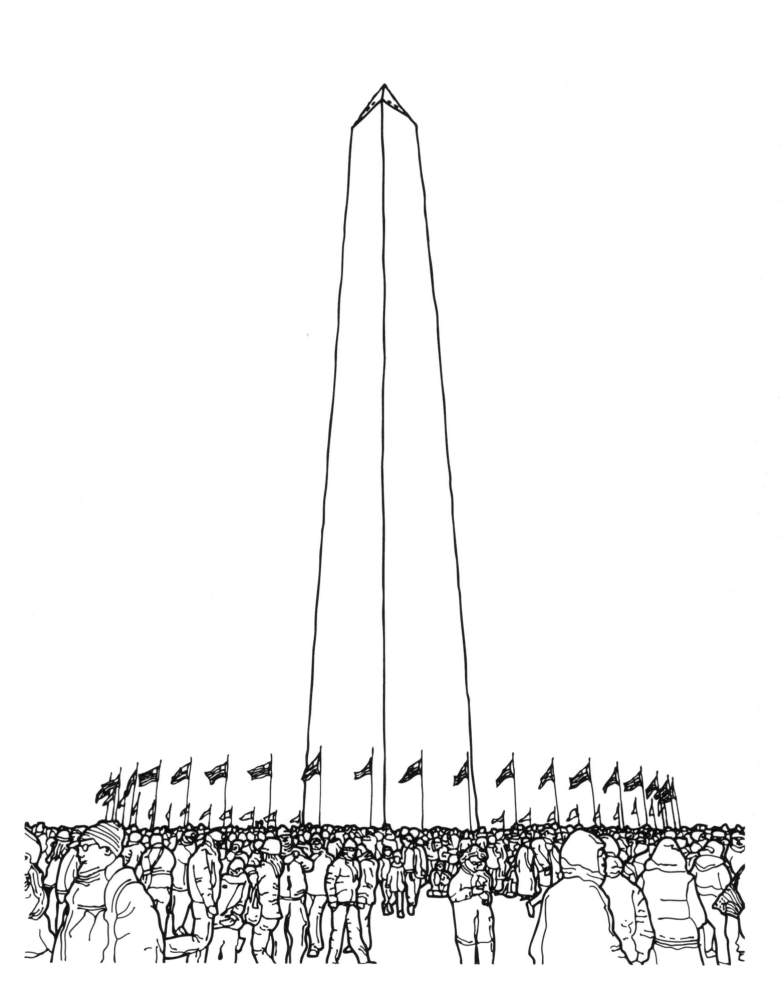

NATIONAL MUSEUM OF AFRICAN AMERICAN HISTORY AND CULTURE

LOCATION: 14th & Madison Drive NW
NEIGHBORHOOD: National Mall
ARCHITECT: David Adjaye

This museum, the Smithsonian's newest, opened its doors in September 2016. It spans five acres and is eight stories tall. The exterior is made of aluminum panels coated in bronze, which are meant to resemble an African basket. Openings in the panel system reveal views of nearby landmarks such as the Washington Monument.

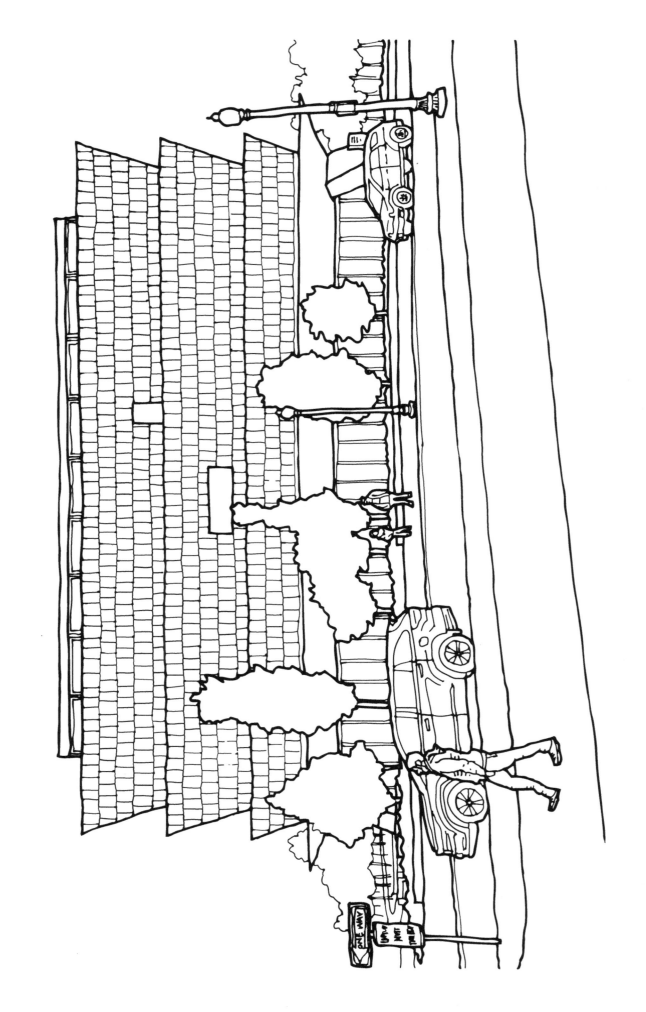

WHITE HOUSE

LOCATION: **1600 Pennsylvania Avenue NW**
NEIGHBORHOOD: **Between Lafayette Square**
and the Ellipse
ARCHITECT: **James Hoban**

Burned in 1814 during the War of 1812 with Britain, the president's house has been renovated and altered many times over the course of history. The Oval Office, located in the West Wing, was designed by architect Nathan C. Wyeth and was added in the early 20th century.

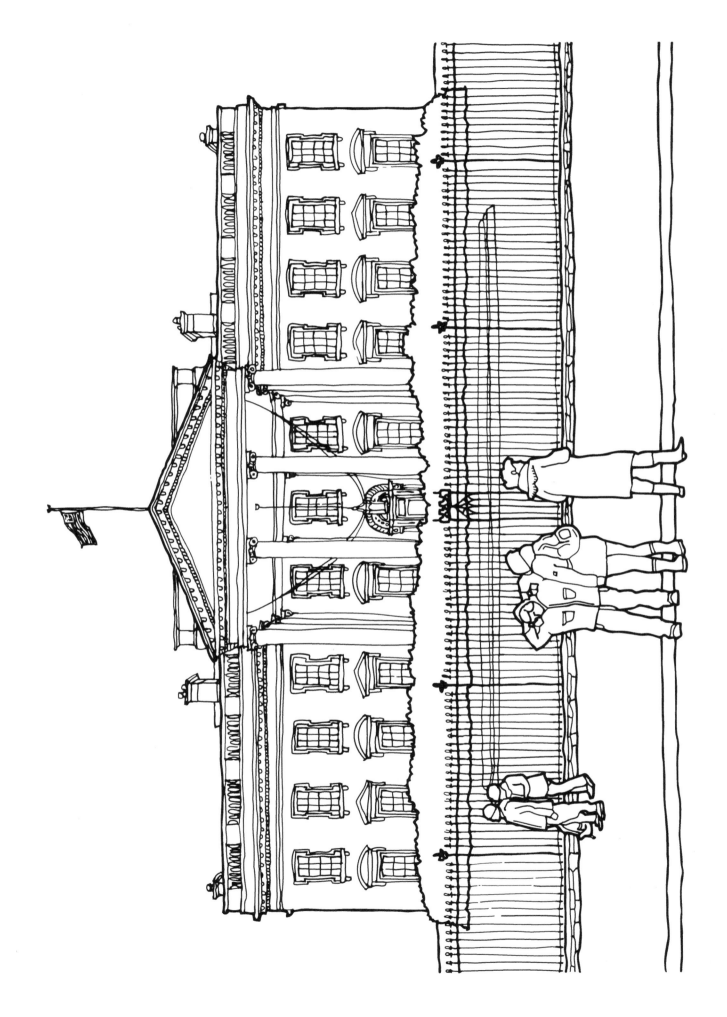

NATIONAL PRESS BUILDING (FORMER FOX THEATRE, LATER KNOWN AS LOEW'S CAPITOL)

LOCATION: 14th & F Streets NW
NEIGHBORHOOD: Metro Center
ARCHITECTS: Rapp & Rapp Architects

Although the National Press Club was founded in 1908, the club had three locations prior to President Coolidge laying the cornerstone at its current location in 1926. Formerly the site of the Ebbitt Hotel, the new National Press Building included a Fox Theatre, later known as Loew's Capitol, for many years until the theater was repurposed. Like the White House, the National Press Club has its own zip code, 20045, one of several large-scale or iconic buildings nationwide with that distinction.

BROWNLEY CONFECTIONERY BUILDING

LOCATION: 1309 F Street NW
NEIGHBORHOOD: Penn Quarter
ARCHITECTS: Porter and Lockie

Listed on the National Register of Historic Places, this is one of the last Art Deco commercial buildings in downtown Washington. Originally built as a family-run candy store and soda shop, the decorative panels and trim work are made of aluminum.

OLD POST OFFICE

LOCATION: **1100 Pennsylvania Avenue NW**
NEIGHBORHOOD: **Federal Triangle**
ARCHITECT: **Willoughby J. Edbrooke**

The Old Post Office was built in 1899 and is the second tallest building in Washington after the Washington Monument, and at 315 feet, this structure rivals London's Big Ben in height (316 feet). Although it was threatened with demolition multiple times, it reopened in 2016 as Trump International Hotel.

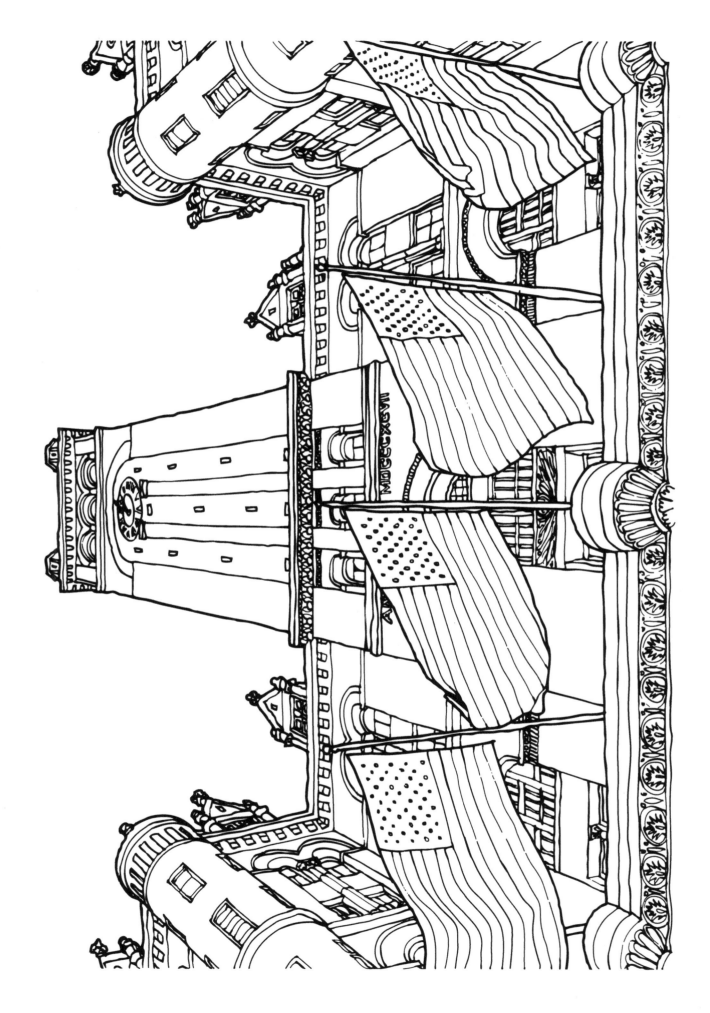

NATIONAL ARCHIVES

LOCATION: **700 Pennsylvania Avenue NW**
NEIGHBORHOOD: **Federal Triangle**
ARCHITECT: **John Russell Pope**

The National Archives houses original copies of the Bill of Rights, the Constitution, and the Declaration of Independence. Other documents there include the Louisiana Purchase Treaty and the Emancipation Proclamation, an executive order issued by President Abraham Lincoln that granted freedom to all slaves in Confederate states. Sculptures known as *Heritage* (left) and *Guardianship* (right) were designed by sculptor James Earle Fraser.

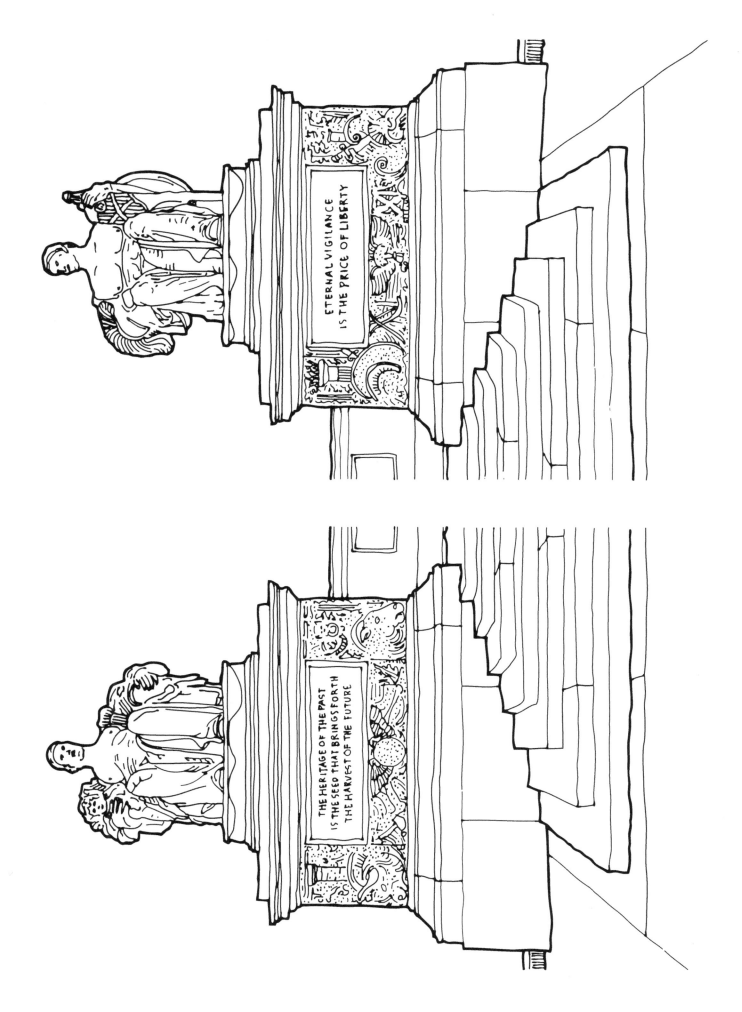

FORD'S THEATRE

LOCATION: 511 10th Street NW
NEIGHBORHOOD: Penn Quarter
ARCHITECT: Charles Lessig

Ford's Theatre is most notably known as the site of President Abraham Lincoln's assassination in 1865 by John Wilkes Booth, an actor who had performed several times at the theater. After the assassination, it was decided that the building would not reopen as a theater, and it was sold as an office building. Nearly 100 years after the assassination, in 1968, Ford's Theatre reopened as a theater.

MADAME TUSSAUDS
(RICH'S SHOE STORE BUILDING)

LOCATION: **1001 F Street NW**
NEIGHBORHOOD: **Metro Center**
ARCHITECT: **Unknown**

This structure was originally the Woodward & Lothrop (Woodies) flagship department store. Later it became the B. Rich & Sons family shoe store until 1961, when the shop relocated just blocks away. During its most recent renovation, hundreds of left shoes, likely display shoes, were found in the basement.

EQUITABLE BANK BUILDING

LOCATION: 915 F Street NW
NEIGHBORHOOD: Metro Center
ARCHITECTS: Frederic B. Pyle
and Arthur B. Heaton

Constructed in 1912, this temple-front building was originally a bank, but like many historic buildings in D.C., it has been home to nightclubs and will soon become a restaurant. While its function may change, efforts are being made to preserve the building's historic architectural elements.

NATIONAL BUILDING MUSEUM

LOCATION: **401 F Street NW**
NEIGHBORHOOD: **Judiciary Square**
ARCHITECT: **Montgomery C. Meigs**

Built between 1882 and 1886, the Pension Building, now the National Building Museum, was constructed in response to the end of the Civil War as a place where veterans could receive their monetary compensation. The exterior of the building was modeled after the Palazzo Farnese in Rome, as can be seen by the semicircular and triangular pediments. The interior of the structure is ornamented by arches and columns like the interior of the Palazzo della Cancelleria, also in Rome.

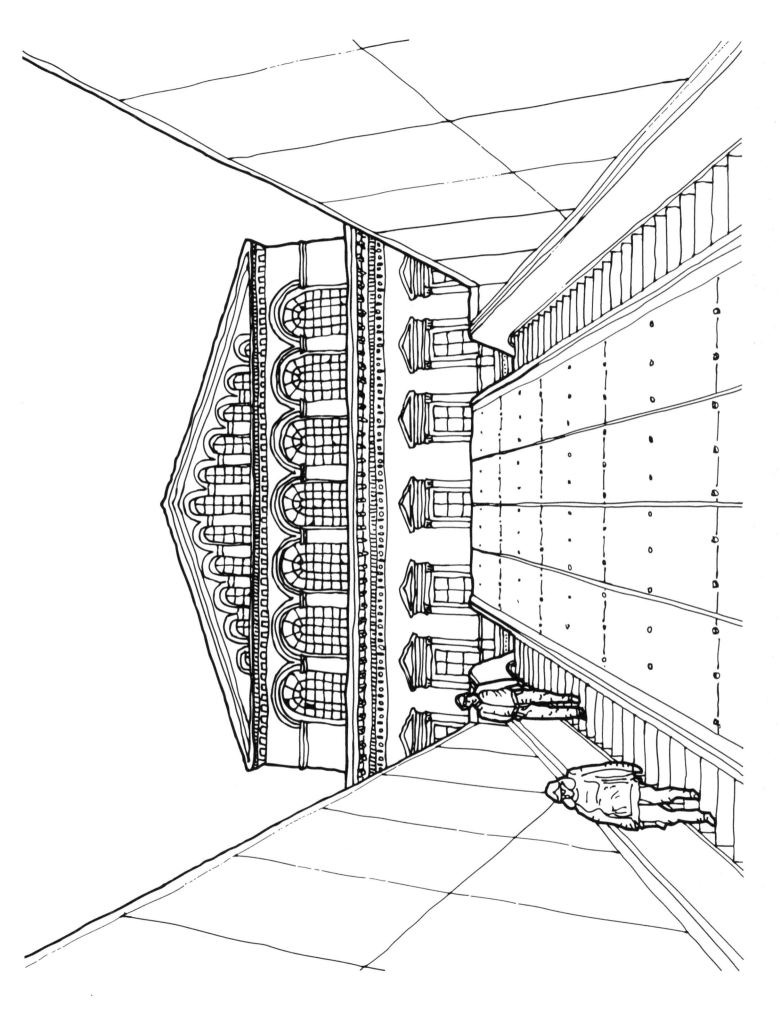

HISTORICAL SOCIETY OF WASHINGTON, D.C. (CARNEGIE LIBRARY)

LOCATION: **8th and K Street NW**
NEIGHBORHOOD: **Mount Vernon Square**
ARCHITECTS: **Ackerman and Ross**

This structure was originally built as a library with funds from Andrew Carnegie. Its Beaux-Arts design is articulated through the arched doorways and windows, as well as its sculptural figures located on the left and right corners of the building's central mass. Although the building has changed over the years, it is currently home to the Historical Society of Washington, D.C., after the City Museum of Washington closed after only a year in operation there.

FRANKLIN SCHOOL

LOCATION: **13th and K Street NW**
NEIGHBORHOOD: **Downtown**
ARCHITECT: **Adolf Cluss**

This structure was originally designed for the District of Columbia public school system. In 1873 the school district won a Medal of Progress award from the Vienna Exposition (World's Fair) for its innovative German "around arch" design.

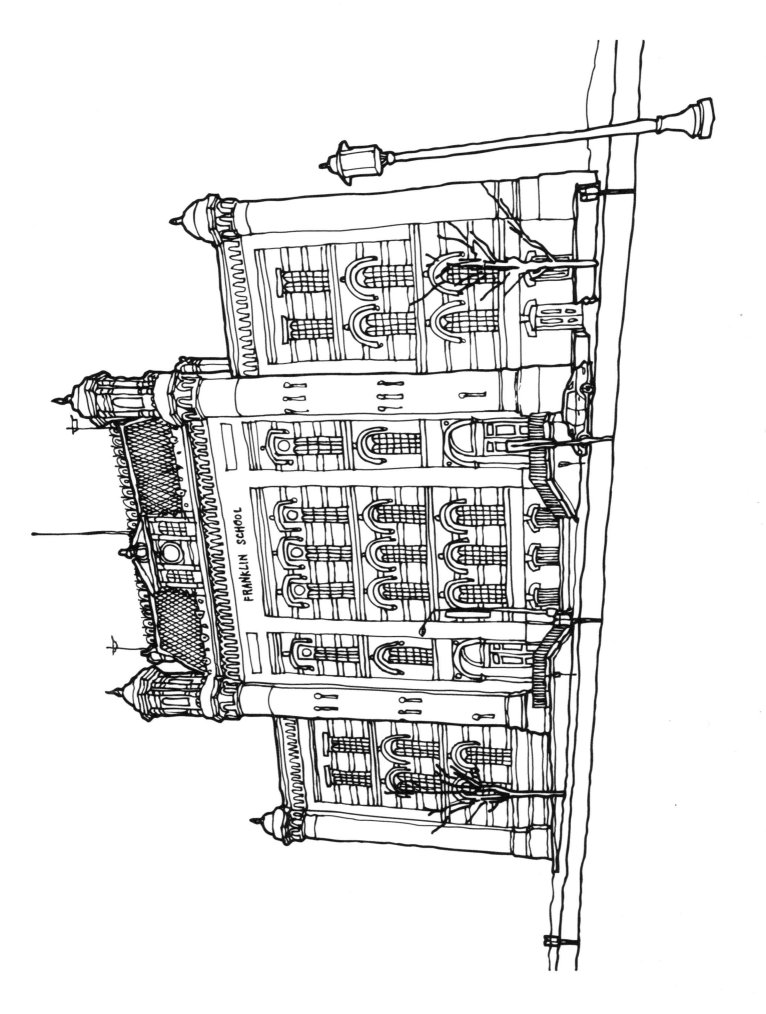

Almas Temple

LOCATION: **1315 K Street NW**
NEIGHBORHOOD: **Downtown**
ARCHITECT: **Allen Hussell Potts**

Originally built in 1930, this Moorish-style building was inspired by the Alhambra, a famed palace in Grenada, Spain. After the land on which the Almas Temple was located was sold, the tile was taken down piece by piece and reassembled at its current location in Franklin Square.

HOWARD THEATRE

LOCATION: 610 T Street NW
NEIGHBORHOOD: Shaw
ARCHITECT: J. Edward Storck

The Howard Theatre first opened to the public in 1910. Its façade combines three architectural types: Italian Renaissance, Beaux-Arts, and Neoclassical. After falling into disrepair in the 1960s and 1970s, the Howard Theatre closed in the early 1980s. It reopened to the public in 2012 after extensive repairs.

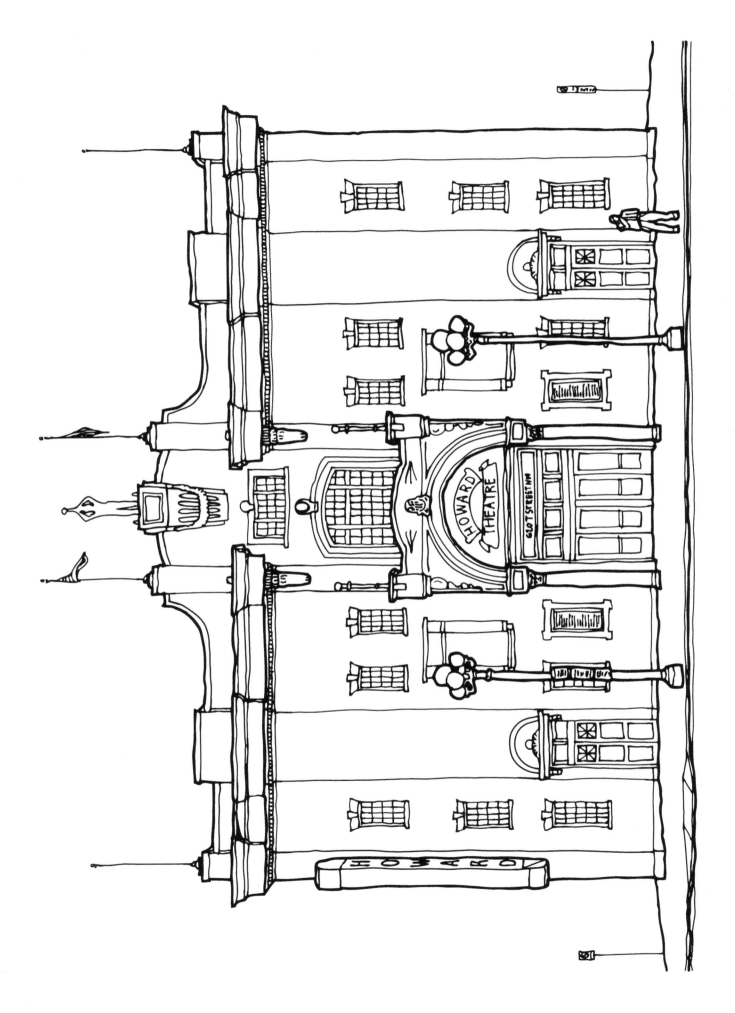

PRESIDENT LINCOLN'S COTTAGE

LOCATION: **140 Rock Creek Church Road NW**
NEIGHBORHOOD: **Petworth**
ARCHITECTS: **John Skirving and William Degges**

Built between 1842 and 1843, President Lincoln used this home during his time in office as a retreat from the White House. This structure utilizes a Gothic Revival design characterized by its pointed arch doorway and diamond-shaped glass panes.

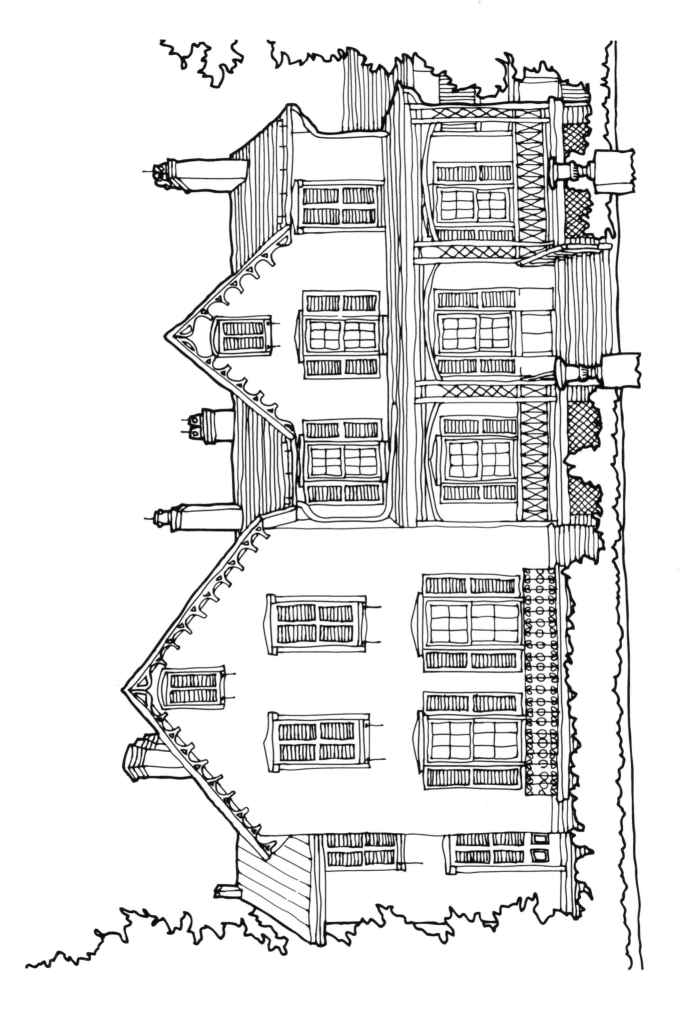

COSMOS CLUB
(TOWNSEND MANSION)

LOCATION: 2121 Massachusetts Avenue NW
NEIGHBORHOOD: Dupont Circle
ARCHITECTS: Carrère and Hastings

Now an exclusive club, this structure was originally home to Richard and Mary Scott Townsend, railroad tycoons from Pennsylvania. Inspired by the French style of Louis XVI, the Townsend Mansion is ornamented by features such as one central structure with two wings and a Rococo-style ballroom.

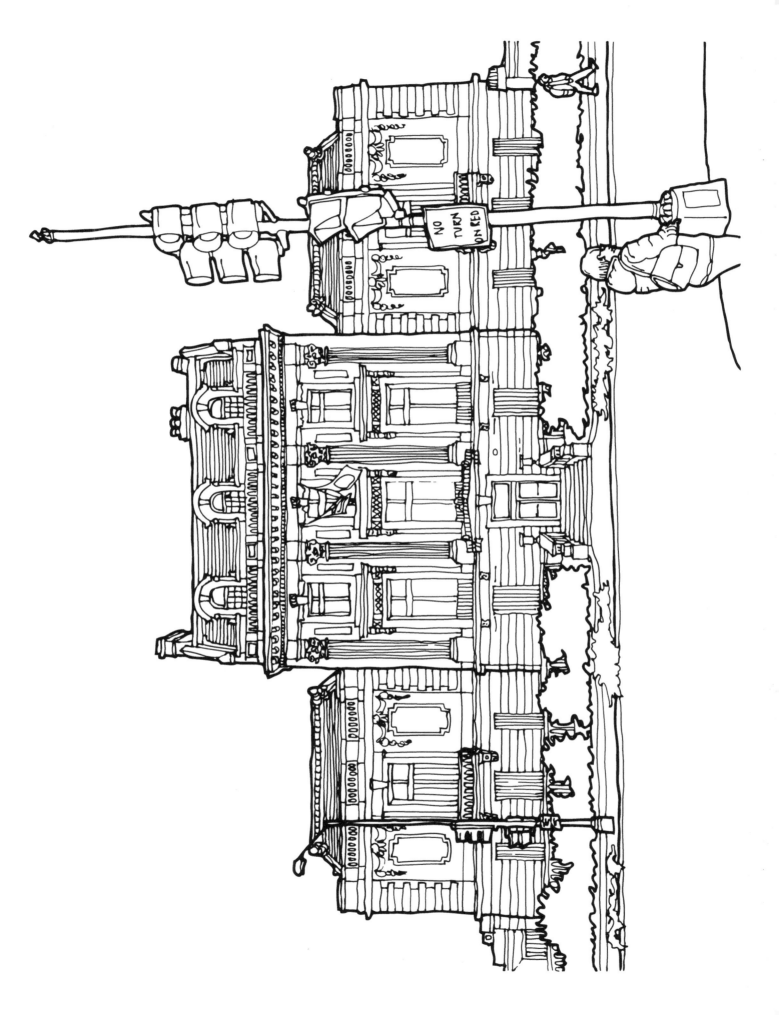

HOUSE OF THE TEMPLE, SCOTTISH RITE OF FREEMASONRY

LOCATION: 1733 16th Street NW
NEIGHBORHOOD: Dupont Circle
ARCHITECT: John Russell Pope

Modeled after the Mausoleum at Halicarnassus, one of the Seven Wonders of the Ancient World, this building incorporates design elements such as the colonnade of 33 columns and the stepped pyramid roof. Other buildings attributed to Pope in the District of Columbia include the Thomas Jefferson Memorial and the National Gallery of Art, West Building.

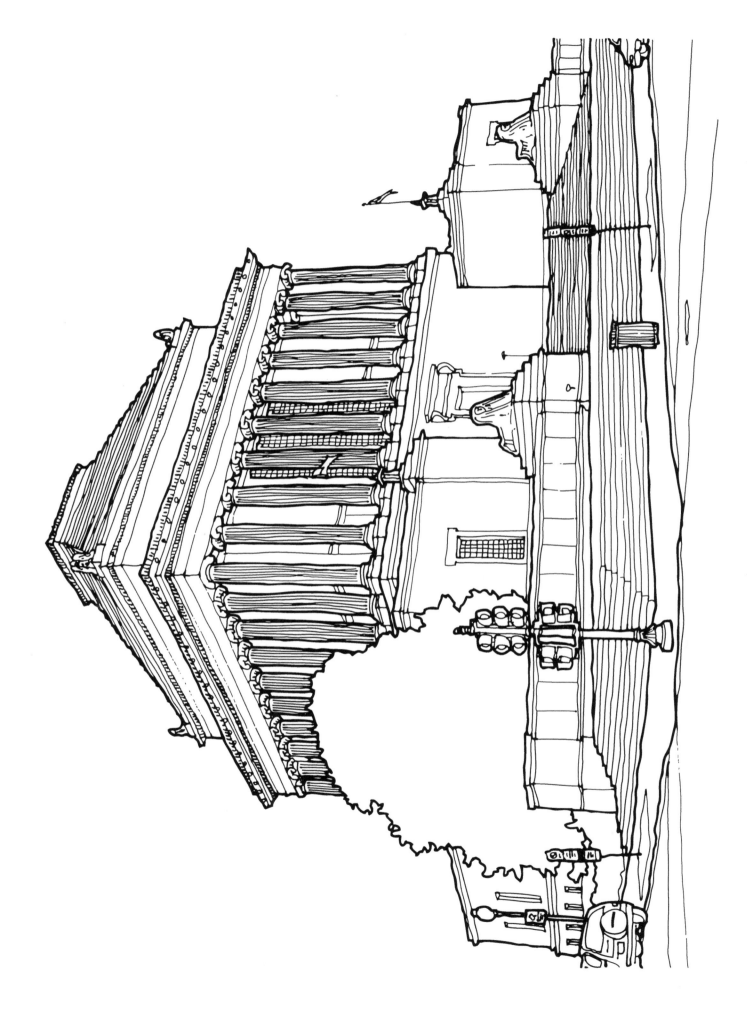

COUNCIL FOR PROFESSIONAL RECOGNITION (FORMER FRENCH EMBASSY)

LOCATION: **2460 16th Street NW**
NEIGHBORHOOD: **Meridian Hill**
ARCHITECT: **George Oakley Totten Jr.**

George Oakley Totten Jr. was a prominent architect in the District of Columbia during the Gilded Age (late 1800s–early 1900s) when millionaires began commissioning lavish homes, many of which are now private clubs, offices, and embassies. In addition to this structure, Totten also designed the current Turkish Embassy and Ambassador's residence.

NICHOLAS T. HALLER HOUSE

LOCATION: 1739 S Street NW
NEIGHBORHOOD: Dupont Circle
ARCHITECT: Nicholas T. Haller

Haller built this home in 1892 to serve as his private residence. In addition to his own home, Haller designed many other homes and apartment buildings around the District of Columbia. Haller also designed his own office building, now called the Warder Building, located near Metro Center.

PATTERSON MANSION

LOCATION: 15 Dupont Circle NW
NEIGHBORHOOD: Dupont Circle
ARCHITECTS: McKim, Mead & White

Made of brick, this Neoclassical structure is characterized by its columns, decorated frieze, and an ornamental design over the doorway. While the use of this building has changed over the years, most notably it was home to President Calvin Coolidge in 1927 while the White House was undergoing renovations. It is currently under construction and will reopen as an apartment building.

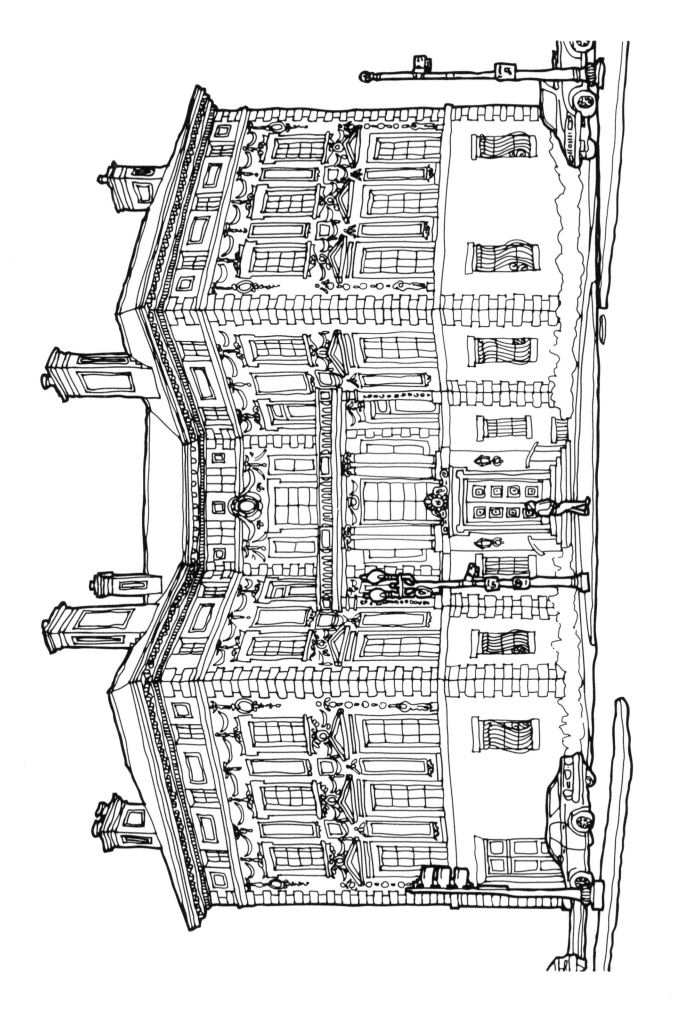

WADDY B. WOOD HOUSE

LOCATION: 2019 Q Street NW
NEIGHBORHOOD: Dupont Circle
ARCHITECT: Waddy B. Wood

Wood designed this home in 1910 for use as his private residence. Wood's most notable work was his design of the Woodrow Wilson House and the main building of the Department of the Interior.

JAMES C. HOOE HOUSE

LOCATION: **2230 Massachusetts Avenue NW**
NEIGHBORHOOD: **Dupont Circle**
ARCHITECT: **George Oakley Totten Jr.**

Built in 1907, this Beaux-Arts townhouse is decorated in terra-cotta and limestone. Unlike many early-20th-century homes that have been converted to museums, embassies, and other institutional uses, this structure is still maintained as a private residence today.

WASHINGTON NATIONAL CATHEDRAL

LOCATION: **Massachusetts and
Wisconsin Avenues NW**
NEIGHBORHOOD: **Massachusetts Heights**
ARCHITECTS: **George Frederick Bodley
and Henry Vaughan**

Considered the highest point in the District of Columbia, the National
Cathedral was begun in 1907, and construction was fully completed only in
1990. Special architectural elements incorporated into the cathedral include
over 10,000 pieces of stained glass and a plethora of stone gargoyles,
including a Darth Vader head!

CPSIA information can be obtained
at www.ICGtesting.com
Printed in the USA
BVHW022321270820
587521BV00007B/19